THE HIP-HOP REVOLUTION

KENDRICK LAMAR

BECOMING THE VOICE OF COMPTON

THERESE M. SHEA

Enslow Publishing
101 W. 23rd Street
Suite 240
New York, NY 10011
USA

enslow.com

Published in 2020 by Enslow Publishing, LLC.
101 W. 23rd Street, Suite 240, New York, NY 10011

Library of Congress Cataloging-in-Publication Data

Names: Shea, Therese M., author.
Title: Kendrick Lamar: becoming the voice of Compton / Therese M. Shea.
Description: New York : Enslow Publishing, 2020. | Series: The hip-hop revolution | Audience: 5 | Includes bibliographical references and index.
Identifiers: LCCN 2018044064| ISBN 9781978509672 (library bound) | ISBN 9781978510296 (pbk.) | ISBN 9781978510319 (6 pack)
Subjects: LCSH: Lamar, Kendrick, 1987—Juvenile literature. | Rap musicians—United States—Biography—Juvenile literature.
Classification: LCC ML3930.L136 S54 2020 | DDC 782.421649092 [B] —dc23
LC record available at https://lccn.loc.gov/2018044064

Printed in the United States of America

To Our Readers: We have done our best to make sure all websites in this book were active and appropriate when we went to press. However, the author and the publisher have no control over and assume no liability for the material available on those websites or on any websites they may link to. Any comments or suggestions can be sent by email to customerservice@enslow.com.

Photo Credits: Cover, p. 1 Joseph Okpako/Getty Images; p. 5 Frazer Harrison/ Getty Images; p. 7 AB1/Adriana M. Barraza/WENN/Newscom; p. 8 Noel Vasquez/ GC Images/Getty Images; p. 11 Chelsea Lauren/WireImage/Getty Images; p. 13 Jim Spellman/WireImage/Getty Images; p. 14 Christopher Polk/Getty Images; p. 17 Joey Foley/Getty Images; p. 19 Johnny Nunez/Getty Images; p. 20 Kevork Djansezian/ Getty Images; p. 23 Kevin Mazur/Getty Images; p. 25 © AP Images; p. 26 Emma McIntyre/Getty Images; title graphics (arrows) Vecster/Shutterstock.com.

CONTENTS

1

A KID IN COMPTON

Kendrick Lamar Duckworth is better known as the rapper Kendrick Lamar. He grew up in Compton, a city in California with a history of gang violence. Kendrick managed to resist the pull of gang life, but he never turned his back on his city. Instead, he became its storyteller, telling the tales the rest of the world needs to know through his music. Some consider him to be the greatest rapper alive today.

Kendrick was born in Compton on June 17, 1987. His parents, Kenny Duckworth and Paula Oliver, had moved there to escape gangs in Chicago, Illinois. They arrived with $500 and their belongings in garbage bags.[1] They stayed in motels and even in their car until they saved enough money for an apartment.

Kendrick Lamar attends the 2017 MTV Video Music Awards in Inglewood, California. Lamar won Video of the Year for his single "HUMBLE."

Unfortunately, Compton had gangs, too. It was hard for Kendrick's parents to stay away from the gang life, but they tried to protect him from it. They kept him busy with activities, such as basketball. But Kendrick, called "Man-Man" by his parents, was an observant child. And there was a lot to observe in Compton. "I was always in the corner of the room watching," he recalled.[2] Many of his childhood memories are about trying to figure out what people were doing and how things worked.

A TALENTED WRITER

Kendrick was a good student. He even read the dictionary for fun. He once amazed a third-grade teacher by using the word "audacity." His mother encouraged him in his schoolwork and urged him to follow his dreams. His father advised him to keep challenging himself. Young Kendrick was especially good at writing. He knew he had a gift when one day he hurriedly did an assignment and received an A. "School was pretty fun for me," he remembered.[3]

A seventh-grade teacher introduced Kendrick to poetry. He loved using certain elements such as metaphors to write poems and lyrics. "You could put all

Early Influences

When he was young, Kendrick listened to Snoop Dogg, Jay-Z, and DMX, among others. He wrote his own raps for their songs. When he was eight, he watched Dr. Dre and Tupac Shakur shoot a video for the song "California Love." "It sparked something," he said. "I always kept thinking about that moment."[4]

your feelings down on a sheet of paper, and they'd make sense to you," he said. "I liked that."[5] Still, he wasn't an instant performer. He had a stutter until middle school. When he was excited, he had difficulty saying certain words.

Many of Kendrick's friends were involved in gangs and shootings. He was close to joining that life himself. He had been shot at and seen murders. Most of his friends from elementary school later ended up dead or in jail. Kendrick said, "There was a split second when I felt what my homeboys were feeling . . . and that's when I knew something

Kendrick Lamar's mother, Paula Oliver, attends the BET Awards in Los Angeles, California, in 2016. Her encouragement helped her son reach stardom.

else had to happen."[6] Kendrick's music was that "something else."

GETTING A RECORD DEAL

By the time he was sixteen years old, Kendrick had been freestyling for eight years. He was rapping under the name K.Dot. In 2003, he released a mixtape called *Y.H.N.I.C.* It got the attention of a lot

Anthony Tiffith (*left*) and Kendrick Lamar attend a basketball game in Los Angeles, California, in 2015. Tiffith gave Lamar his first record deal.

of people in Compton, and soon, of people in the music business.

A friend suggested that Kendrick perform for Anthony "Top Dawg" Tiffith, owner of the record label Top Dawg Entertainment. Kendrick performed with no prepared material, just rapping what came into his head for two hours. Tiffith was struck by Kendrick's maturity: "What impressed me was

"That's when I knew something else had to happen."

how advanced Kendrick was at 16 years old. He spoke from an adult perspective every time he touched the mic."[7] Tiffith offered Kendrick a record deal.

INTO THE
INDUSTRY

Working with a record label helped Kendrick Lamar stay on the music path. He released another mixtape in 2005 called *Training Day*. He got the chance to work with other talented young rappers. Lamar also performed as an opening act for West Coast rapper The Game. He was even featured in The Game's single "The Cypha."

After working with Lil Wayne, Lamar put out a mixtape called *C4* in 2009. It was inspired by Lil Wayne's work. That same year, Lamar became part of the rap group Black Hippy, along with rappers Jay Rock, Ab-Soul, and Schoolboy Q.

Lamar was making a name for himself. Around this time, his friend (and later manager) Dave Free suggested that Lamar stop rapping as K.Dot and start performing

Kendrick Lamar and The Game (*right*) perform onstage on January 18, 2015, in Los Angeles, California. The Game has praised Lamar's "real rap."

under his real name. Lamar decided to use his first and middle name. However, his friends never stopped calling him "Dot."

In late 2009, the album *The Kendrick Lamar EP* came out. It's said to be his first album because it's the first under a record label. It featured fifteen tracks that focus on subjects Lamar would return to many times, such as family, drugs, and gangs.

"DESTINED FOR GREATNESS"

Kendrick Lamar released another mixtape, called *Overly Dedicated*, in 2010. He was coming into his own style and losing some of the style that he had copied from other rappers. He introduced Compton through the music.

On one track, "Ignorance Is Bliss," his lyrics are rapidly rapped over the sounds of string instruments. One of his heroes, Dr. Dre, heard it on YouTube.

Dr. Dre took notice because the track was different than other rap songs. "It gave him

"It gave him both sides of the story in Compton, the victim and the aggressor."

Dr. Dre

Dr. Dre, born André Romelle Young, was one of the founders of gangsta rap, a style that focuses on life in violent inner cities. In 1986, he started the rap group N.W.A. with Eazy-E and Ice Cube. Their 1988 album, *Straight Outta Compton*, was a hit. Dr. Dre became a producer.

both sides of the story in Compton, the victim and the aggressor, and that's something he'd never seen," Lamar explained. "Every time you hear gangsta rap, everybody's the aggressor, there's really no vulnerability, and I bring that other side of the story because I've been on both ends."[1]

Dr. Dre watched a video of Lamar talking about his music and was impressed by his passion. "You just knew this guy was destined for greatness."[2] Dr. Dre signed Kendrick Lamar to his record label Aftermath.

Dr. Dre (*left*) and Lamar pose at the Rock and Roll Hall of Fame Induction Ceremony. N.W.A. joined the Hall of Fame in 2016.

Jay-Z (*left*), Pharrell Williams (*right*), and Lamar attend the Grammy Awards in 2014. Kendrick has earned the respect of many artists in the music industry.

EDUCATING BY ENTERTAINING

Dr. Dre worked with Kendrick Lamar to produce Lamar's next album, 2012's *good kid, m.A.A.d city.* The album cover shows a young Lamar, two of his uncles, and his grandfather. Lamar was the "good kid" who lived in the "mad" city of Compton. The stories he told through the album's tracks were true. He painted a picture of life on the streets. He gave details about people, places, and events. One of these was seeing a shooting at a hamburger stand.

Lamar explained "m.A.A.d." in the album name stands for two phrases. One is "my angry adolescence divided," which has to do with the violence he saw as a child. The other is "my angel's on angel dust."[3] This meaning has to do with his bad experience with drugs. He turned his back on drug use ever since. Other songs touched on the harmful effects of alcohol. Producer Pharrell Williams, who worked on the album, said, "His ability to entertain while educating, without ever being preachy, is amazing."[4] Lamar was just describing his life growing up.

The album had great reviews. It debuted at number two on the US Billboard 200 music chart and has sold more than 1.7 million copies.[5]

THE GOOD KID GETS BETTER

The album *good kid, m.A.A.d city* was a hit, appealing to more than just hip-hop fans. Many thought it was a classic from the start. To promote the album, Lamar began a world tour. He played twenty-three shows and appeared at thirty-seven national and international festivals. He performed on the television shows *Saturday Night Live* and *Late Night with Jimmy Fallon*, too. A short film based on the album was made and shown at the Sundance NEXT movie festival in Los Angeles, California.

WRITING IT ALL DOWN

Lamar began keeping a diary. "I didn't want to forget how I was feeling when my album dropped, or when I went back to Compton," he said.[1] He filled several notebooks with writing and drawings. He used these as part of his creative process. He explained, "I spend 80 percent of my time thinking about how I'm going to execute, and that might be a whole year of constantly jotting down ideas, figuring out how I'm going to convey these words to a person to connect to it. . . . Then, the lyrics are easy."[2] When Lamar was ready to work on his next album, his notebooks helped him.

Lamar waves to the audience in Cincinnati, Ohio, during the 2012 Under the Influence of Music tour. He performed with Wiz Khalifa, Mac Miller, and many others.

GOING BACK HOME

Because of his success, Lamar found himself worried about becoming a different person. In an interview with comedian Dave Chappelle in 2017, Lamar recalled, "Everything was moving so fast. I didn't know how to digest it. The best thing I did was go back to the city of Compton, to touch the people who I grew up with and tell them the stories of the people I met around the world."[3]

In an article in *Vanity Fair* magazine, Lamar described his neighbors' amazement over how their lives could be reflected so well in his songs: "They literally cried tears of joy when they listened to it—because these are people who have been shunned out of society. But I know the kinds of hearts they have; they're great individuals."[4]

"They literally cried tears of joy when they listened to it."

Lamar wasn't sure at first how he wanted his music to be labeled. It wasn't gangsta rap exactly. He realized he had a gift for expressing himself truthfully. That became his label for his music: honest self-expression. He wanted others to learn to express themselves, too.

Lamar is honored with the key to Compton on February 13, 2016. He continues to give back to his community and help the people there.

Lamar accepts the Grammy Award for Best Rap Album for *To Pimp a Butterfly* from rapper Ice Cube on February 15, 2016.

BUTTERFLY FLIES HIGH

Kendrick Lamar's 2015 album was called *To Pimp a Butterfly*. It didn't look back on his past. It focused on his experiences as a young black man in the United States today. He talked about success and fame and the challenges that came with them. He reflected on subjects such as racism and police violence. Again, Lamar showed his vulnerable side in his lyrics. And again, he

Kendrick Lamar and Tupac Shakur

Lamar greatly admires rapper Tupac Shakur, who died in 1996. On the track "Mortal Man" on *To Pimp a Butterfly*, he asks Shakur questions about how to stay grounded and about the future for African Americans. Shakur "answers" using quotes from an old interview he did.

showed off his agility as a rapper. A *Time* magazine review noted Lamar didn't stick to the beats of the song. Instead he used them as "canvases—he doodles on and around them."[5]

In 2016, the album was nominated for eleven Grammy Awards and won Best Rap Album. In fact, Kendrick Lamar won the most Grammys of any artist that year. On the award show, he performed the songs "The Blacker the Berry" and "Alright" with a mix of spoken word, jazz, and African dance.

In March 2016, Lamar released a number of tracks that hadn't been finished on time for *To Pimp a Butterfly*. Some of the songs included jazz, funk, and soul sounds. The collection was called *untitled unmastered*. It debuted at the top of the Billboard 200 chart.

AT THE TOP
OF THE GAME

4

In April 2017, Kendrick Lamar released his fourth album, *DAMN*. In the opening track, "BLOOD.," Lamar asks the question "Is it weakness or wickedness?" He explores the battle within himself about decisions he and others have made. The songs "HUMBLE." and

A True Track

Lamar's favorite song on *DAMN*. is "DUCK-WORTH." It is based on his father's prevention of a robbery at a neighborhood KFC restaurant. Lamar said the song is about recognizing that everyone has a different point of view about an event and about the importance of trying to understand someone else's viewpoint.

Lamar performs during Rihanna's Annual Diamond Ball in New York City in 2017. The benefit raised $5 million for charity.

"PRIDE." explore these competing feelings. "HUMBLE." became his first number-one song as a solo artist on the Billboard 100 chart. Also, on the album, Lamar worked with the singer Rihanna and with the band U2.

Lamar said that listening to the album from the first track to the last tells a story. Listening to it in reverse, from the last track to the first, is a different experience. "I don't think the story necessarily changes, I think the feel changes," he added. "Both of these pieces are who I am."[1]

DAMN. was another hit, topping the charts in both the United States and Canada. It won the 2018 Grammy for Best Rap Album, while "HUMBLE." won Best Rap Song as well as Best Music Video.

THE FIRST PULITZER PRIZE-WINNING RAPPER

In 2018, Lamar produced a soundtrack for the movie *Black Panther*. The superhero movie featured a mostly black cast. Its soundtrack featured many African artists as well as different kinds of music, including R&B, pop, soul, and a kind of South African house music called gqom. Lamar performed several songs, including "All the Stars" with the singer SZA. The result was a diverse musical experience. The album debuted on the top of the Billboard 200 chart. In June 2018, Lamar was asked to join the music branch of the Academy of Motion Picture Arts and Sciences.

In April 2018, Lamar received big news. His album *DAMN.* had won the Pulitzer Prize for Music. The judges had listened to a hundred works. They said *DAMN.* was chosen for the respected prize because it told moving stories about the complicated lives of today's African Americans. They had all agreed it deserved the honor.

Kendrick Lamar was the first rapper to win the Pulitzer Prize. It had been given to classical or jazz musicians in the past. The award meant hip-hop was finally valued as other kinds of music were. Pulitzer Prize finalist Ted Hearne called Lamar "one of the greatest living American composers, for sure."[2]

Lamar shakes hands with Columbia University president Lee Bollinger after accepting the 2018 Pulitzer Prize for Music for the album *DAMN*.

A FUTURE WITHOUT LIMITS

In 2018, Kendrick Lamar made his acting debut in the television series *Power*. His friend, rapper 50 Cent, produces and stars in the show. Lamar played a homeless man and received good reviews for his acting. This role shows that, even at the top of the rap game,

Lamar speaks during the MTV Movie Awards on April 9, 2016. He uses his celebrity to bring attention to important social issues.

Lamar isn't done challenging himself. He might even go back to school one day. An A student in high school, he said he "could have went . . . should have went" to college. He said, "It's always in the back of my mind. It's not too late."[3]

For now, Lamar is focused on his career and, as always, Compton. He no longer lives there, but he returns to keep in touch with those he left behind. He said, "I can't get rid of the 20 years of being with my homies, and knowing what they go through. I can't throw that away."[4] Telling their stories—and his own—continues to be essential to him.

> "I can't get rid of the 20 years of being with my homies, and knowing what they go through."

Thanks to Kendrick Lamar, people outside of the hip-hop culture are finally seeing the music as more than just lyrics; hip-hop is a reflection of real pain. His songs aren't just clever words over catchy beats. His music has become a bridge between communities.

TIMELINE

1987 Kendrick Lamar Duckworth is born in Compton, California, on June 17.

2003 Lamar releases a mixtape called *Y.H.N.I.C.*

2005 Lamar releases the mixtape *Training Day*.

2009 He releases the mixtape *C4*.

2009 The album *The Kendrick Lamar EP* comes out.

2010 Lamar releases the mixtape *Overly Dedicated*.

2012 Dr. Dre signs Lamar to his record label Aftermath.

2012 The album *good kid, m.A.A.d city* is released.

2015 The album *To Pimp a Butterfly* is released.

2016 The album *untitled unmastered* debuts.

2017 Lamar releases the album *DAMN.*

2018 Lamar produces the soundtrack to the movie *Black Panther*.

2018 Lamar wins the Pulitzer Prize for Music for *DAMN.*

CHAPTER NOTES

CHAPTER 1: A KID IN COMPTON

1. Josh Eells, "The Trials of Kendrick Lamar," *Rolling Stone,* June 22, 2015, https://www.rollingstone.com/music/music-news/the-trials-of-kendrick-lamar-33057.

2. Ibid.

3. Andres Tardio, "Here's What Kendrick Lamar's Childhood Was Like," MTV News, July 6, 2015, http://www.mtv.com/news/2205410/kendrick-lamar-childhood.

4. Tom Barnes, "The Story Behind How Kendrick Lamar Became the King of West Coast Rap," Mic, May 27, 2015, https://mic.com/articles/119372/the-story-behind-how-kendrick-lamar-became-the-king-of-west-coast-rap#.MwW3eMweW.

5. Eells.

6. Lisa Robinson, "The Gospel According to Kendrick Lamar," *Vanity Fair,* June 28, 2018, https://www.vanityfair.com/style/2018/06/kendrick-lamar-cover-story.

7. Ibid.

CHAPTER 2: INTO THE INDUSTRY

1. Victoria Ahearn, "Kendrick Lamar Says Dr. Dre Was Drawn to His Fresh Approach to Gangsta Rap," *Canadian Press,* October 25, 2012, Questia, https://www.questia.com/newspaper/1P3-2800174081/kendrick-lamar-says-dr-dre-was-drawn-to-his-fresh.

2. Lisa Robinson, "The Gospel According to Kendrick Lamar," *Vanity Fair,* June 28, 2018, https://www.vanityfair.com/style/2018/06/kendrick-lamar-cover-story.

3. Chris Martins, "Kendrick Lamar: 'm.A.A.d.' Stands for 'Me, an Angel on Angel Dust,'" *Spin,* October 19, 2012, https://www.spin.com/2012/10/kendrick-lamar-maad-stands-for-angel-dust.

4. Robinson.

5. Keith Caulfield, "Kendrick Lamar Scores Third Million-Selling Album in U.S. with 'DAMN.' *Billboard,* April 6, 2018, https://www.billboard.com/articles/columns/chart-beat/8295475/kendrick-lamar-damn-sells-million-copies.

CHAPTER 3: THE GOOD KID GETS BETTER

1. Josh Eells, "The Trials of Kendrick Lamar," *Rolling Stone,* June 22, 2015, https://www.rollingstone.com/music/music-news/the-trials-of-kendrick-lamar-33057.
2. Lisa Robinson, "Kendrick Lamar on What Drives Him and the Album That Changed His Life," *GQ Australia,* August 27, 2018, https://www.gq.com.au/entertainment/celebrity/kendrick-lamar-on-what-drives-him-and-the-album-that-changed-his-life/image-gallery/9810b64db84c1782fb617b1c6544c34b.
3. Dave Chappelle, "Kendrick Lamar," *Interview,* July 12, 2017, https://www.interviewmagazine.com/music/kendrick-lamar-cover.
4. Lisa Robinson, "The Gospel According to Kendrick Lamar," *Vanity Fair,* June 28, 2018, https://www.vanityfair.com/style/2018/06/kendrick-lamar-cover-story.
5. Jamieson Cox, "REVIEW: Kendrick Lamar's *To Pimp a Butterfly* Is an Angst-Filled Anthem for Blackness," *Time,* March 17, 2015, http://time.com/3747392/kendrick-lamar-to-pimp-a-butterfly-review.

CHAPTER 4: AT THE TOP OF THE GAME

1. Madeline Roth, "Kendrick Lamar Tells Us Why He Loves Playing *DAMN.* in Reverse," MTV News, August 24, 2017, http://www.mtv.com/news/3032281/kendrick-lamar-damn-reverse-interview.
2. Joe Coscarelli, "Kendrick Lamar Wins Pulitzer in 'Big Moment for Hip-Hop,'" *New York Times,* April 16, 2018, https://www.nytimes.com/2018/04/16/arts/music/kendrick-lamar-pulitzer-prize-damn.html.
3. Josh Eells, "The Trials of Kendrick Lamar," *Rolling Stone,* June 22, 2015, https://www.rollingstone.com/music/music-news/the-trials-of-kendrick-lamar-33057.
4. Lisa Robinson, "The Gospel According to Kendrick Lamar," *Vanity Fair*, June 28, 2018, https://www.vanityfair.com/style/2018/06/kendrick-lamar-cover-story.

GLOSSARY

aggressor One who attacks another.

agility The ability to move quickly and easily.

audacity The quality of being confident and daring.

convey To communicate.

debut To provide a product to the public for the first time.

execute To produce a work of art.

freestyle To rap using lyrics mostly made up on the spot about any subject that comes into one's head.

metaphor A phrase that is used to refer to another thing in order to suggest that they are similar.

mixtape A collection of recorded songs that is often given away for free in order to build a fan base.

producer One who is in charge of making and sometimes providing the money for a record.

unmastered Not edited.

vulnerability The quality of being open to harm.

FURTHER READING

BOOKS

Aswell, Sarah. *Kendrick Lamar: Rap Titan*. Minneapolis, MN: Essential Library, 2018.

Cummings, Judy Dodge. *The Men of Hip-Hop*. Minneapolis, MN: Essential Library, 2018.

Morse, Eric. *What Is Hip-Hop?* La Jolla, CA: Black Sheep, 2017.

WEBSITES

Biography: Kendrick Lamar
www.biography.com/people/ kendrick-lamar-21349281
Read more about the star's rise to fame.

Kendrick Lamar
www.kendricklamar.com
Check out news, tour info, photos, music, and videos on Lamar's official website.

INDEX